Fire and Thunder of the Bard

Fire and Thunder of the Bard

POETIC MESSAGES OF DIVINE SPIRITUAL HEALING

JANINE PALMER (SILVER MOON) CHT

– A JP SILVER MOON SERIES –

Fire and Thunder of the Bard
Copyright © 2018 by Janine Palmer (Silver Moon) CHT. All rights reserved.

No part of this publication may be reproduced, stored in a retrieval system or transmitted in any way by any means, electronic, mechanical, photocopy, recording or otherwise without the prior permission of the author except as provided by USA copyright law.

The opinions expressed by the author are not necessarily those of Stonewall Press.

Published in the United States of America

ISBN: 978-1-64460-057-3 (*sc*)
    978-1-64460-056-6 (*e*)

Library of Congress Control Number: 2018964557

Published by Stonewall Press
4800 Hampden Lane, Suite 200, Bethesda, MD 20814 USA
1.888.334.0980 | www.stonewallpress.com

Poetry
19.01.08

Other Books by Janine Palmer

MAIN BOOKS

Divine Heretic – Standing Holy
Divine Heretic – In Christ Consciousness
Divine Heretic – Sacred Scribe
Divine Heretic – Mystical Fire
Divine Heretic – Alchemist
Divine Heretic – Hierophant
Divine Heretic – Hidden Keys
Magic Quill – Sacred Sword

GENRE SPECIFIC BOOKS
(Material Pulled from Main Books)

Energy Healing Wisdom
Spiritual Healing Wisdom
Divine Healing Wisdom
Rising Above Dogma
For Romance
Heart Speak
Book of Worthiness
Apocalypse of Worthiness
Scriptures of Worthiness
Shamanic Energy Medicine
Sacred Shamanic Whispers

This book is dedicated to my family with deep love and to all the people who inspired me to write and to all poets and writers. The poetry contained herein is an acknowledgement to the healing powers of writing. Writing about the importance of processing and releasing emotions becomes artistic expression. Energy needs to flow. These tales are about releasing those blocks. Trust the process of unfolding and spiritual evolvement.

Blessings, love and light.

Janine Palmer (Silver Moon) CHT

Contents

Foreword 1

Sacred Temple 3

Glimpses of Soul 11

Mystical & Sacred 21

Divine Wisdom 31

Energy Healing 41

Fire of Transformation 51

Spiritual Alchemy 61

Worthiness & Wings 75

Blessed Be Our Magic 85

Deeper Truth 95

Mirror, Mirror 107

Battle Scars & Shedding Skins 117

Treasure & Keys 127

Suffering & Shadow 137

Whispers from the Heart 149

Light Through the Cracks 157

Spoken from the Soul 171

Beyond Belief 183
Metaphoric Light 197
Perspectives 207

About the Author 225

Foreword

THIS LITTLE BOOK REFLECTS GLIMPSES of experience and the wisdom gained from them. It reflects wounds, and the effects of the wounded who wound. It speaks of energy healing and forgiveness. It speaks of spiritual alchemy and the ascension of the spirit and the soul. It speaks of opening the door of the heart to love.

It speaks of battle scars and shedding skins and shells. It speaks of sacred temples and the fire of transformation. It speaks of rising above and moving beyond judgment, the spiraling, higher path to freedom through love and healing and releasing what does not serve. It speaks of the power of forgiveness. It speaks of things mystical and sacred. It speaks of magic.

It speaks of angels and dragons and divine love. It speaks of mirrors, treasures, keys and the mystical. It speaks of shadow and perspectives. It speaks of spirit, heart, soul and light. It speaks of deeper truth beyond belief and hidden keys. It basically shares the depth of love revealed by life experiences.

Sacred Temple

Who transcribes the language of my soul? I do. It's a process of unfolding I am dancing with, remembering and embracing. Who reflects me? I do. Who loves me? I do. I am here to unfold myself.

Sacred Temple

I now wear my sword on my back and use it to cut away any negativity which does not serve me.

I still have immense compassion, I just direct more of it toward myself now.

Sacred Temple

There comes a time to take
care of yourself and that time
is now.

Sacred Temple

Some Christians seem to be afraid of Yoga?! Yoga is ancient medicine for body, mind and soul. Different types and levels. There is nothing to be afraid of. It's a way of caring for your temple.

But so many people are conditioned and programmed in fear and guilt and shame and falsehoods, to their determent, which moves them farther away from Source.

To know the love of the Christ and Jesus without the trappings of dogma is amazing and an important part of Ascension.

Sacred Temple

Something higher works through people, including me, to share messages for healing and upliftment.

Sacred Temple

The Divine works through me,
through my writing, through
my heart and my soul.

Sacred Temple

Glimpses of Soul

When the poet is consumed by the poem or the poetry, mystery flows, healing flows, beauty flows, light flows and love flows.

To pour from the vessel of Oneness which is light, at the same time being drawn back to it, to become it more fully again.

The poet pours from him or herself, knowledge, wisdom, pain and remedy, as well as messages from the Mystery.

The poet is the poetry, shared upon the pages of the book of their life. When anyone shares from their heart and soul, there is beauty and magic woven in between the lines.

For those who are treasure seekers, there is always something profound to discover.

Glimpses of Soul

The beat of her drum took her to other worlds where deep healing took place with the help of many beloved guides.

Glimpses of Soul

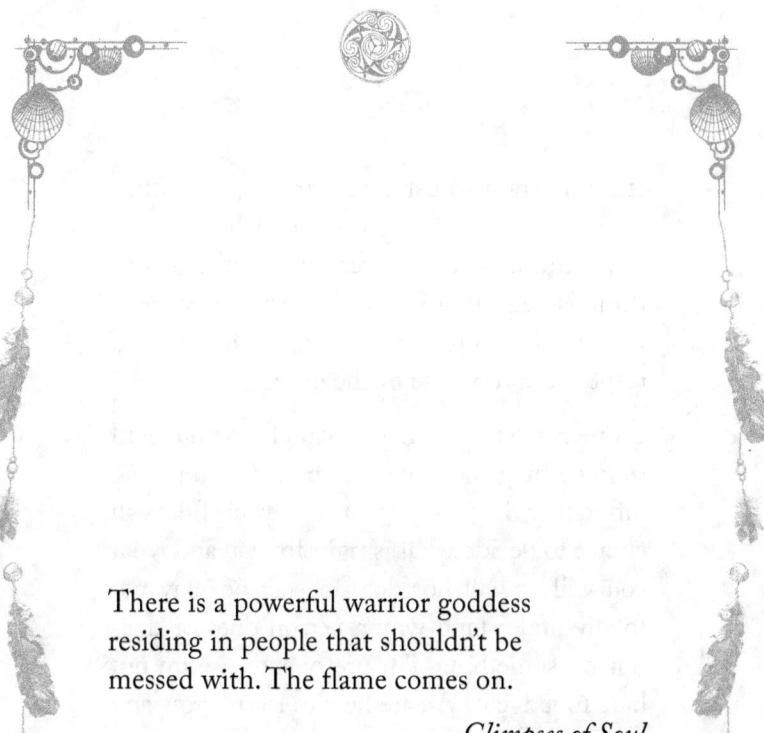

There is a powerful warrior goddess residing in people that shouldn't be messed with. The flame comes on.

Glimpses of Soul

It's important to listen to a friend when they speak, it's about being open and honest and respectful if they are offering something they think is helpful or just saying what they feel. It's equally important to try to honor and respect the response of the other.

If one person says what they prefer with regard to something and that you should do something differently, it's up to you and your free will choice to decide what is right for you and what you will or will not do. One person may not totally understand why a person does or does not do something. I'm pretty sure we are not here to judge it. We are here to learn, grow and evolve. We are here to learn to let shit go.

When we judge or put down what someone does or doesn't do, it is often a reflection of something unresolved in us. When find fault with people or their behavior, it might be reflecting something within us that needs attention. Of course we don't stand by for atrocities and do nothing, but we also don't need to micro manage things we might not fully understand to fit into some tidy little box of our ideas about how we think things should be.

Also, it's so terribly important to remember that we never have all the facts about anyone or anything so we are always functioning from and reacting to limited information. Reacting to one side of any story is a recipe for disaster.

I speak frankly and directly with power and force when I need to or with kindness and compassion when I need to. I know who I am and I know what my mission is. I will speak directly and passionately about what I believe I need to. I will not make stuff up and fake it in order to accommodate anyone due to expectations.

I give myself permission to be me, however powerful or forceful or however meek and compassionate. The choice is and shall remain, mine.

Glimpses of Soul

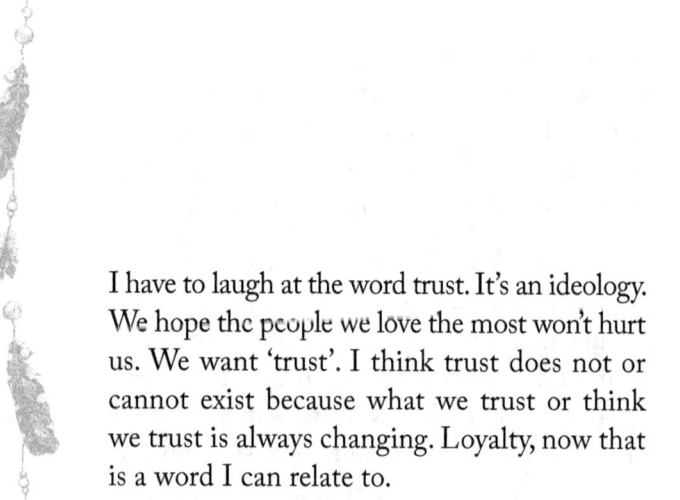

I have to laugh at the word trust. It's an ideology. We hope the people we love the most won't hurt us. We want 'trust'. I think trust does not or cannot exist because what we trust or think we trust is always changing. Loyalty, now that is a word I can relate to.

Glimpses of Soul

We are loyal to love because we are love. When love stops being demonstrated and shared its part of the flux of change and people move on. It doesn't mean they can't be trusted and it doesn't mean they are not loyal. We must first be loyal to ourselves and not expect anyone else to make us happy.

Glimpses of Soul

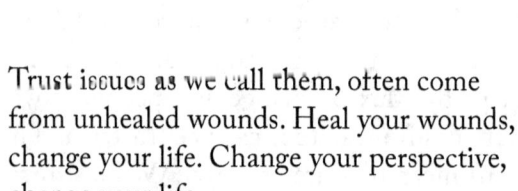

Trust issues as we call them, often come from unhealed wounds. Heal your wounds, change your life. Change your perspective, change your life.

Glimpses of the Soul

Mystical & Sacred

The Rain

She dances under dark clouds,
She drinks the rain alive,
The gray clouds make her happy,
Through storm clouds her soul thrives.

So cherished are all raindrops,
For the life which they provide,
You might find her dancing in it,
From the rain she does not hide.

To feed the trees and flowers,
To feed the heart and soul,
To nurture by nature's cycles,
Through sacred streams which flow.

Mystical & Sacred

Credentials might be far more or less than we think they are. As a divine being of light on this planet, your credentials are part of your energetic blueprint of love and worthiness. Show the world what you've got.

Mystical & Sacred

Relationships are forms of
art and we are the artists.

Mystical & Sacred

We need to meet and love each aspect of our soul so we can create a life that reflects the colors which shine from every beautiful facet of our soul.

Mystical & Sacred

Sometimes we get pushed out of places we're not really supposed to be, and that's okay. We just need to let it go with love and smile with gratitude for what we learned and contributed.

When you try to be present but you continue to be meet with contrariness, it's a sign to fade out of that energy and elevate into something higher.

Give yourself permission to flow and let the power of your true authentic self swirl around you in waves of colorful beauty.

Mystical & Sacred

My gratitude for so many things is something it seems difficult to put the right words to. Words are not enough to describe what is felt in the heart.

Mystical & Sacred

When I sit in a room, which is not influenced by inspiration, a room whose demeanor and style is not injected with personality and flavor of art and artistic expression, it feels lonely and cold.

I love it when a room speaks to me and tells me stories as a book would. I love a room that encourages thought, reflection and creativity. I love a room that boldly states that it is welcoming, sacred space.

Mystical & Sacred

Divine Wisdom

Blossom in elegance to the tune
of your innocence remembered

Divine Wisdom

It's only ever about what is learned from the experience and what you do with what you learn.

Divine Wisdom

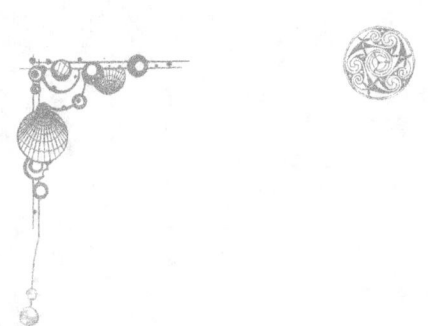

When falsehoods are flung at you, it's a test. If you know they aren't true, you don't need to react or even respond. It's an attempt to draw your energy. The question is, what would you be feeding? Ego or soul?

Divine Wisdom

This is a time of being tested.
Notice your progress.

Divine Wisdom

Without awareness we stumble through the fog. To be aware, we must be open. The light enters through an open lens.

Divine Wisdom

Sometimes compassion and kindness is mistaken for weakness when in fact it is the exact opposite.

Divine Wisdom

Misunderstandings have always been and continue to be problematic on this planet, due to limited information.

Misunderstandings create situations that feel hurtful or unfair, when perhaps they were not intended to.

Misunderstandings often cause us to be hurtful toward others, knowingly or unknowingly, in defense of ourselves, due to something unhealed in ourselves.

This is often a realm of suffering. The question is, how can we help each other rise out of it? What do our actions and thoughts create?

Divine Wisdom

There is a pureness many don't understand but are always drawn back to.

Divine Wisdom

Energy Healing

Roots and branches and veins.
What flows through them? Life.
Life must flow. Energy must flow.
Blocks must be cleared.

Maintenance is required. Remove
the energetic blocks, even in the
form of thoughts or perceptions,
so love may flow where it needs
to go.

Energy Healing

Some thought her bravery was weakness. Perhaps they hadn't been to the depths of hell or the heights of heaven she had, so their judgement had no power over her.

Their behavior was a test to reflect her response or reaction back to her. If she was paying attention, she could see where she needed strengthening, healing or release.

She could also see her progress and when she was no longer triggered. In gratitude she smiled. Her sword and her dragon smiled too.

Energy Healing

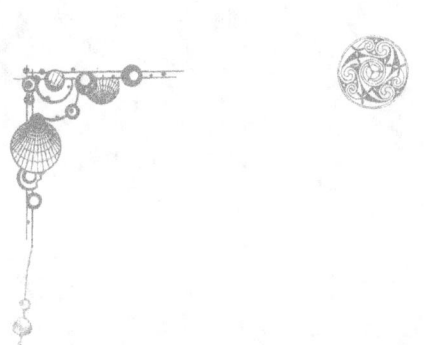

One does not mend the tears in the soul by feeding the ego. Mending the tears calls for immense self-love, the love beyond the realm of ego.

Energy Healing

Victim of the system? How about, No. We all have free will choice, and we are all in charge of how we react to the tests and illusions of earth school. It is so very important to be aware that we constantly react to limited perspectives and lack of knowledge.

Energy Healing

We are tested in ways and on levels our human conscious mind doesn't understand, but our soul does. We are challenged to step up and speak our truth and so we should.

We cannot fix something from the lower vibrational energies which created it. As we do the work to heal ourselves individually and release old pain and unhealed wounds, we raise our vibration and we can do the work that is needed from there.

We do not help our ancestors by staying stuck in hatred and pain. We are not victims we are in the process of becoming victorious. Sometimes we have to let go of things to create new things. Any of us here only has limited perspectives of things.

If we could see what was happening from a broader view and what people are learning from these horrific challenges, we would understand it differently, but we don't. The land needs healing, the people need healing, the animals need healing and that we can do. Peace and blessing. A'ho.

Energy Healing

To move beyond jealousy for some is a monumental task. It often keeps people stuck in a realm of suffering which then spews out onto others.

We are tested here to move beyond and rise above. In order to do that we must love ourselves and check to make sure we are taking care of and nurturing our inner child.

We would benefit greatly from leaning how to detach. We would benefit from our own compassion.

Energy Healing

Perhaps it is high time we did away with running programs of victim mentality, if we wish to rise. It's important to remember that by our choices, decisions, actions and reactions, we become the cause of our creations, not just the effects of them.

It's our responses to our life experiences which determine what patterns are activated. When this is understood, perhaps we will not willingly give our power away and suffer unnecessarily and/or cause others to. What is your recipe for taking your power back?

Energy Healing

Fire of Transformation

When we go through deeply intense traumas, we don't come out of them the same person that we were before they happened. Friends and loved ones might not understand how we have been changed by events. They might judge and shun through misunderstanding or fear.

When we rise from the ashes as a phoenix to rebirth ourselves and build a new life, there is a power no words can describe. It's the energetic light of a warrior who has survived. As we apply that power to our lives in creative ways, sometimes people become jealous and try to put out our brilliant light or they want that light to shine only in their direction.

As we fly above and they try to grab hold of our feet and pull us back down, our wings are always mighty and strong enough to raise us out of those trying situations. Those who have rebirthed themselves from the ashes discover this.

Fire of Transformation

Dealing with people isn't easy. Many of us don't realize, what feels hurtful from others , is not about us. Getting to a place where we aren't bothered by what others say and do can be a difficult road, but the destination is worth the treacherous journey. It's a powerful elevation.

Fire of Transformation

She spoke of good dragons which helped burn away the cords of falsehoods and illusion. Seraphim Angels, Dragons, higher dimensional beings, the fiery ones. Forged in sacred fire.

Fire of Transformation

It's the hurt or perceived hurt which is often the fuel or the catalyst for change. It's about endeavoring to make a positive difference on some level, even if it's only from limited understanding. Intention and action create change.

Fire of Transformation

Hating anyone or anything is giving your power or energy to it, just saying. We are challenged to rise above. It's part of ascension. Rising above the illusion all around us. Exit the Matrix.

Fire of Transformation

Don't give your power away
to limited perspectives.

Fire of Transformation

We raise the vibration of the collective when we raise it in ourselves. We cannot fix issues from lower vibrational energies of hated, judgment and fear. We must share love and kindness. It's why we are here.

Fire of Transformation

You are no one's whipping boy. Those who endeavor to pick apart and find fault with everything you do or say are not yet recognizing their own unresolved issues and ego is running their show.

Ego often reflects undeveloped or unhealed aspects. People love to try to make their issues about someone else. Observe, step away, don't get drawn in. Your reaction feeds their programs. Do people change, or do vibrations change?

Fire of Transformation

Spiritual Alchemy

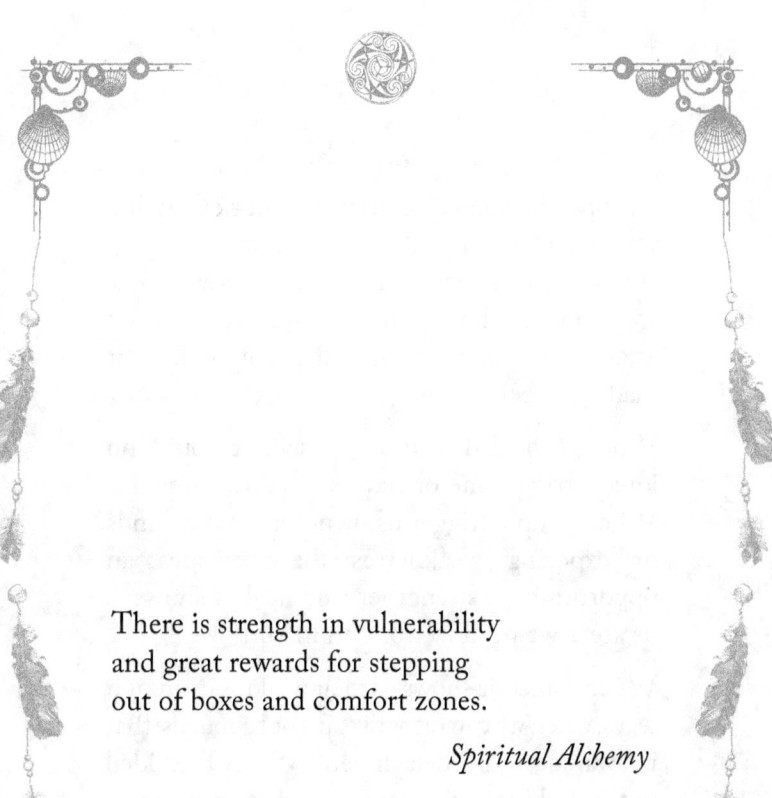

There is strength in vulnerability
and great rewards for stepping
out of boxes and comfort zones.

Spiritual Alchemy

Cutting the source of negativity out of my life wasn't enough. I had to change my thoughts about what happened. It was about awareness, with no attachment to it. That includes no attachment to how I felt about it or how it made me feel.

When I healed that in myself, it could no longer trigger me or have any power over me. When people trigger us by poking old wounds or exposing weaknesses that becomes an opportunity to strengthen and heal. It shows us areas we need to work on in ourselves.

When someone shows us their wounds in unkind ways, when we can recognize it's not about us, that is awareness and detachment. When I decided not to hold it against anyone, what they did or how I perceived what they did, then I walked out of a self-made cell. Those people need more love not less. But we are not targets for treachery.

To send blessings, love and prayers is very healing to both parties on some level. Holding onto resentment is toxic. All of these things help us to grow and evolve and raise our vibration, when we are ready.

Spiritual Alchemy

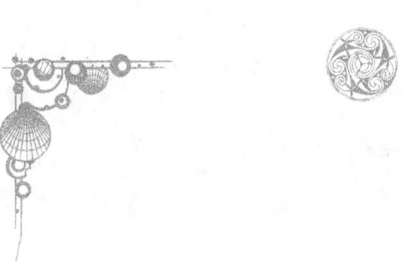

There is a time for humility and
a time to stand in your power.
There is a time when both are
balanced.

Spiritual Alchemy

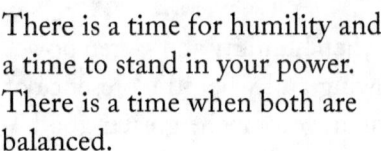

It is beautiful when humility and sacred power become a knowing and when the presence of both is working in you for the greater good.

Spiritual Alchemy

She said, 'I removed from myself the weapons they threw in their ignorance, anger and pain. I removed the daggers and the darts and the knives, and I used them as pens to write with, to transform the fuckery with the magic of words.

I used the energy of my own love and compassion to shine light on dark events for transmutation. I used their weapons of darkness to write love spells of light. Many of them thought I was stuck in the pain of the wounds when I was actually in the throes of alchemy.'

Spiritual Alchemy

Say hello to my sword, which
is brilliant at cutting cords.

Spiritual Alchemy

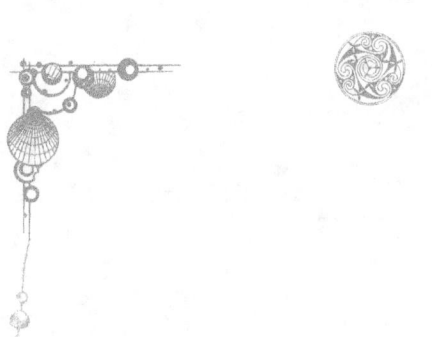

There comes a time to stop trying to accommodate everyone else and just be your authentic self. Carve your own path. Now.

Spiritual Alchemy

The shite we encounter fuels
the chemical process.

Spiritual Alchemy

We are all in each other's lives for a reason. Some of us are friends who can help each other through things, to help each other heal and rise above, because we are brave enough to try. To do so we must open our hearts.

Some supposed friends won't turn out to be friends at all, but rather extremely challenging tests, which was probably divinely orchestrated. We might not come to this realization unless and until we rise above and move beyond certain ideologies, programming and mindsets.

This lovely life is a series of initiations, whether we realize it or not. We will be tested and hopefully there will come a point where we begin to see our progress. We might notice our progress by our responses or reactions to things and to triggers. Things spiral around to retest us.

When things which used to bother us or hurt us or trigger us, no longer do, or not as much, we begin to see where we have healed old wounds or strengthened weaknesses. It happens by degrees as there are many layers. When we can get to a point where we no longer hold things against ourselves or others, we are much more in our power.

We become more powerful and we do it through love, through letting go and through forgiveness. These are superpowers and so is detaching. Attachment causes suffering. Some people are not ready to let go of the pain. Somehow it has become part of their identity. They feed it and it feeds them. Even attachment to thoughts about things and ideologies and opinions can keep us stuck in suffering.

The suffering is our own creation, regardless of what anyone 'did' to us. Sometimes people make choices and do things to have experiences to learn from. Even though they are unkind and inconsiderate, often it was not about us but about the other person who made that choice. We must have been deemed strong enough on a higher level to have had that experience with that person. We are now tested on the lower level to find the wisdom woven in between the pain.

The suffering is our own creation because we have the choice of how to respond or react and how to rise above, move beyond or whether to carry immense burdens. It's all choice.

We create our realities by our thoughts, decisions, actions and reactions. If we don't like something we have created, or habits and patterns we have gotten into, only we can change that.

Also, it is hugely helpful to discover programs we are running which do not serve us and which keep us stuck and release them. This requires soul searching, prayer and meditation, honesty with self, and being proactive to do energy healing work.

You must love yourself enough to step out on that path of healing and awakening to shed the skins and break out of the shells. To do this you must be brave enough to open your heart. There is strength in vulnerability and there is victory from surrender.

Spiritual Alchemy

Worthiness & Wings

What is magical to me might not be magical to someone else. I am called to discover my magic and to create my magic, even if no one else understands why.

Worthiness & Wings

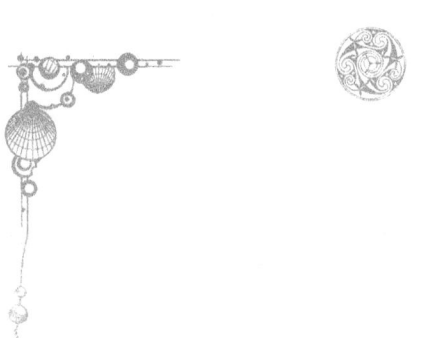

Maybe it's not about how you suffer(ed) or how much you suffer(ed), but about how you changed your perspective about suffering in order to move beyond it.

Worthiness & Wings

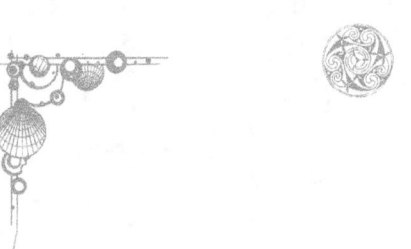

If they feel the need to point out your flaws and weaknesses and put you down in any way, it's a very good indication that there is something unresolved within them, and that there are parts of themselves they have not accepted or healed.

Worthiness & Wings

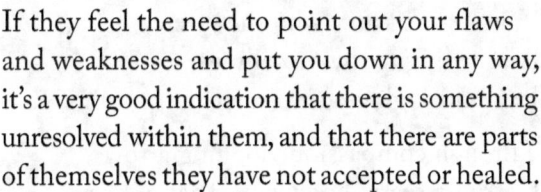

Elegance Unfolding

Through service of love now given,
Offered through our Grace,
Through tests and tasks ongoing,
By initiations we must face.

Goddesses on earth awakening,
Who didn't know who they were,
Awakening to divine callings,
Here through grace to serve.

Through compassion, dodging arrows,
Carrying secret knowledge they are keys,
Sacred vessels of divinity,
And how do we honor these?

As illusion is disassembled,
As we return to grace,
When compassion is stronger than ego,
We welcome sacred space.

Worthiness & Wings

It's okay to have friends.
Every being deserves it,
requires it. It's part of the
learning experience.

How do you nurture it, like
any seed, to blossom and
grow once it sprouts out of
the darkness?

Worthiness & Wings

Sometimes we bend over backwards to accommodate others because of their ideas, demands or expectations. When we are strong, sometimes our energy is too much for people, especially if one or the other is not open.

Sometimes compassion and kindness is mistaken for weakness when in fact it is the exact opposite. When we are flexible and work with people they often think they can just push us around of take out their issues on us.

It has happened to me many times with many people. So it becomes a learning experience where I must ask myself, 'What is this trying to show me or to teach me?' It might just be to step away from what doesn't serve me. It's not about anyone being right or wrong.

When people are unkind it is a reflection of their unresolved issues. People are at different levels of awakening and awareness and if where they are with that conflicts with your forward movement, it might just be time to step away.

Give yourself permission to be authentically you, no matter how fiercely compassionate your are, which many people won't even recognize. Many won't or don't recognize or acknowledge how fiercely strong the warrior who stands tall in you is. How strong and courageous you are in the face of the ignorance swirling all around you. The time is only ever now. You are love.

Worthiness & Wings

Blessed Be Our Magic

Everyone needs a friend and
what a blessing it is to be one.

Blessed Be Our Magic

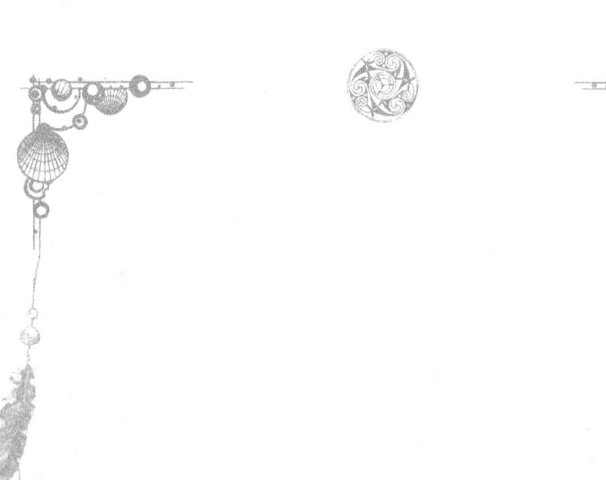

When our efforts are acknowledged, it inspires us to do more. When we are filled, It inspires us to give.

Blessed Be Our Magic

How powerful is the
magic of kindness?

Blessed Be Our Magic

~ What gets triggered in you?
~ Why is it necessary to point out perceived flaws in others?
~ Why would it ever be necessary to put another down?
~ Where does it come from?
~ How does it serve?

When we have not walked in another's shoes or felt their feelings, then we probably wouldn't understand what paths they take to navigate life to elevate to the next level.

There is so much unknown to us about anything or anyone. When shunned by anyone, be very aware the issue is with the one who shuns and not with you.

However, if we are paying attention, there is always something we can become aware of about ourselves which might need to be shifted. Let that beautiful energy flow.

Blessed Be Our Magic

Magic words are, please and thank you.
Magic words are, I love you.
Magic words are, I forgive myself and I forgive you too.
Magic words are, I'm sorry.
Magic words transform feelings, thoughts and energy.
Magic words can heal.

Blessed Be Our Magic

There was a darkness that worked through him. Once recognized, all I could do was bless him.

Blessed Be Our Magic

In some ways she was too powerful for him. It was the divine masculine in her. He didn't understand what it was. She didn't fit in his idea of a woman's role.

Blessed Be Our Magic

He was able to see and feel her magic, something in her which many didn't not understand. It was the energetic balance of the twins.

Blessed Be Our Magic

Deeper Truth

What speaks to my soul most deeply is direct, honest communication, two ways, back and forth. It requires bravery, trust and vulnerability. However, so often when we have done that, someone has found a way to use it against us and made us think we can't trust. We must always allow ourselves to be open and authentic.

People show us who they are and how they fit into our lives. If they cannot function from a place of honor, we can bless them and leave them where they are to heal effects of their traumas and wounds, not to create more of it in our lives.

We must remain open to continue to trust and leave a light on for love which presents itself in many forms. By the way, love can get past those walls you erected. Thoughts and fears are another issue. When would now be a good time to take your power back?

Deeper Truth

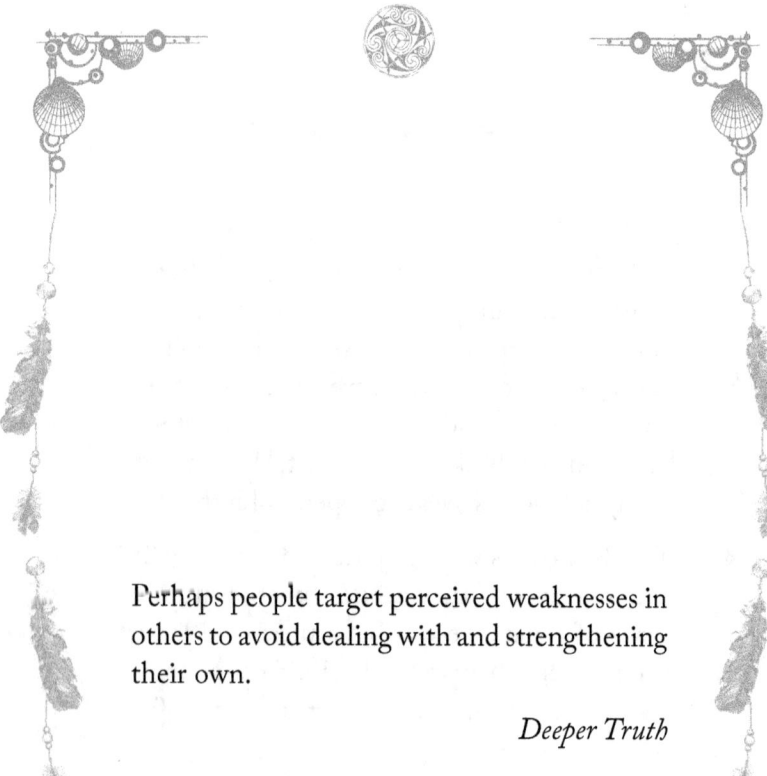

Perhaps people target perceived weaknesses in others to avoid dealing with and strengthening their own.

Deeper Truth

Sometimes people make derogatory comments about others because they can't see the truth about what they are attacking, or they can and they are trying to put out a light.

Deeper Truth

We go through gauntlets which make us stronger. It's what we learn from the experience that matters. It's about what wisdom we take away from the experiences.

Sometimes there are benefits gained from stories told, and how glorious it is when we realize are not our stories.

Deeper Truth

An honest or pure one does not look for weak spots in people in which to thrust a weapon. That would be wounded or unhealed one, or a self-righteous one who doesn't see God, or the Creative Source of love, in self and others. This life school experience is a healing journey and everyone is at different levels of advancement.

Deeper Truth

This place will test the patience of a saint!

Deeper Truth

Communication is a Master Key many people don't seem to know how to use. Welcome to Fuckery.

Although sometimes the communication is about what is expected of you and about what hoops to jump through, and not about true and honest feelings and releasing what doesn't serve.

What would happen to the world if people moved beyond jealousy, wrath and fear?

Deeper Truth

There have been times when negative energy has been directed at me that was disruptive and I've had to cut it out of my space. Times when I gave chance after chance for that to be healed and for people to be respectful.

Often they have not been able to do so, forcing me to become stronger. Tempers flare and rule people sometimes, and emotions and the toxicity of wounds spew out. I've been shown too many times that I cannot trust it when it's a repeating pattern. I've let people back in, then something triggers them and they spew out nasty words which are uncalled for.

We often come to learn that we can't trust recurring triggers and uncontrollable outbursts, but it doesn't mean we don't care about the person just because we love ourselves enough to no longer allow it in our space.

Certain behaviors are destructive and we are not targets. We come to a place where we will not allow that or the opportunity for that, in our space, our sacred space. We often learn these things the hard way.

Often people have no clue what we have endured and suffered because of them, because of their suffering they have not let go of. It is because I love myself and honor myself that I cannot and will not allow certain people back in, at least on certain levels.

I give myself permission to be strong and remain strong. I give myself permission to be in peace and to cut negativity out of my sacred space. I give myself permission to heal. I give myself permission to release what doesn't serve my highest good. I give myself permission to open my heart to love again. I give myself permission to create.

Deeper Truth

Mirror, Mirror

They say life begins at the end of your comfort zone. Oh what a glorious thing it is to step out of the box and then shred it and burn it, to move beyond belief and into knowing.

Mirror, Mirror

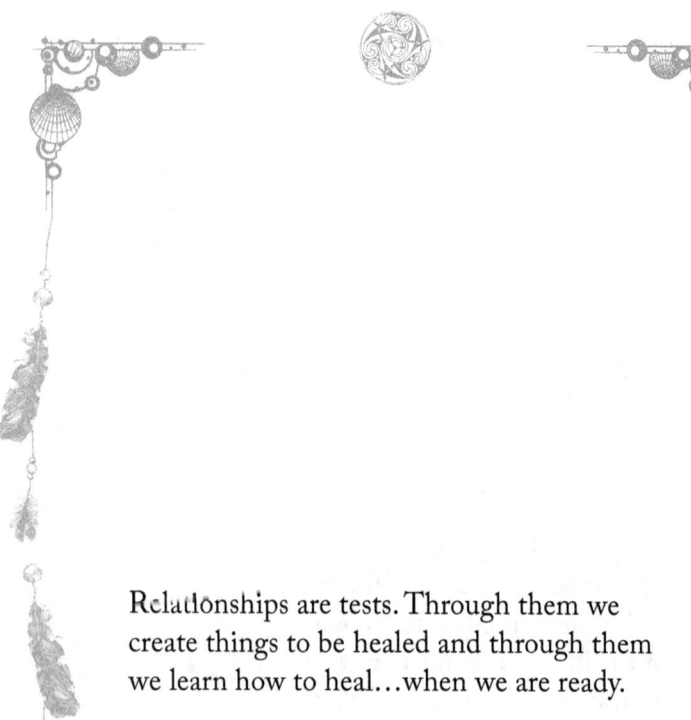

Relationships are tests. Through them we create things to be healed and through them we learn how to heal…when we are ready.

Mirror, Mirror

We must be able to accept ourselves more fully in order to be able to accept others more fully.

Mirror, Mirror

Want to feel more love?
Give more love.

Mirror, Mirror

Be very aware when anyone says something unkind which might feel hurtful or which might attempt to trigger you. You will notice your progress by your reactions or lack thereof.

Many are speaking from the limited knowledge they possess, even intuitive people. No one knows everything about anyone or what has been written and agreed upon. Many attempt to trigger or harm others due to their own pain and unresolved issues.

If/when anyone focuses on an aspect of negativity or what appears to be negative, they are likely functioning from their own unhealed issues, no matter how pure. They might seem to like to point out what they perceive as faults in others, perhaps instead of resolving, healing or strengthening their own. Be aware.

Mirror, Mirror

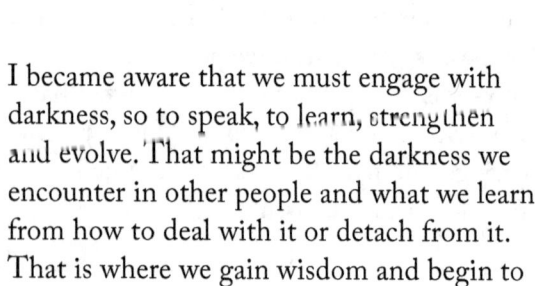

I became aware that we must engage with darkness, so to speak, to learn, strengthen and evolve. That might be the darkness we encounter in other people and what we learn from how to deal with it or detach from it. That is where we gain wisdom and begin to remember who we are.

Mirror, Mirror

All this posturing for position has left us bereft of the very thing we hope to restore. Oneness.

Mirror, Mirror

Perhaps people belittle us and try to make us feel shame because on some level they are intimidated by the brilliance of our light.

Sometimes we aren't aware of our own light. Others are aware of it and sometimes they try to squash it. Just saying...

Mirror, Mirror

Battle Scars & Shedding Skins

Part of her armor gone from the battles of life, but she soldiers on surrounded by the naked truth of divinity.

Battle Scars & Shedding Skins

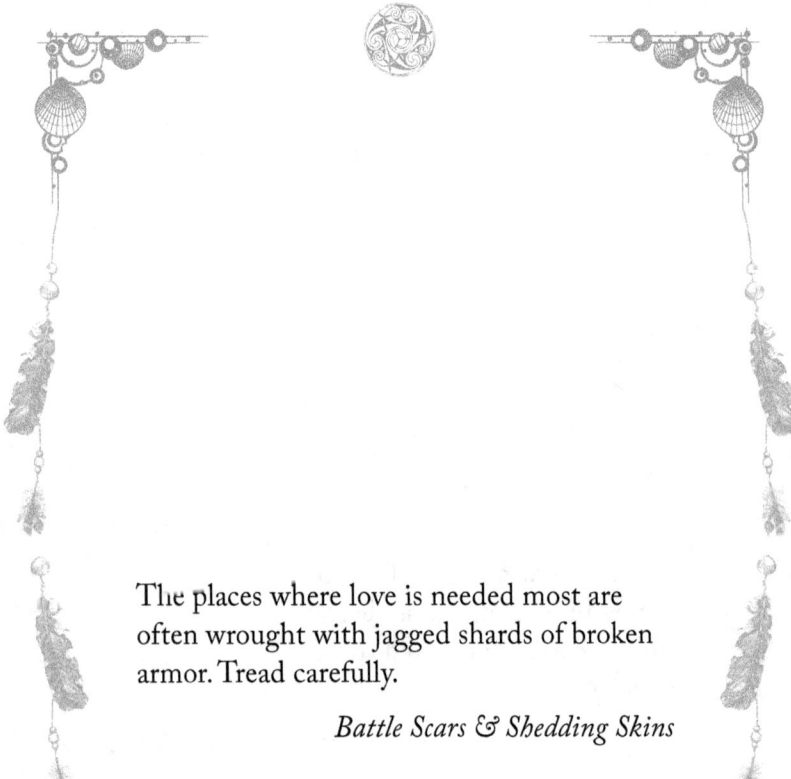

The places where love is needed most are often wrought with jagged shards of broken armor. Tread carefully.

Battle Scars & Shedding Skins

It takes strength be able to feel and process, without being too hard on ourselves. It's okay to be human and to let feelings flow, verbally or in writing. Others should not dictate what that is for us. We navigate these levels in our own divine time. Some will extend a hand to us, to help us or for us to help them. Some will knock us down and kick us when we're down and later we will laugh out loud. We will laugh because of how much stronger we became.

Naysayers serve a purpose. It seems there is great truth to the belief that people can only accept you as much as they accept themselves. A neutral place of non-judgement and non-reaction is a beautiful and rare place. It's a place where love originates and where love blossoms.

What I write is for Ascension. Mine. But it's also for the collective as we all must rise together. That is why it's necessary to help one another rather than hurting one another.

When we stop being offended we are rising. Beyond self-righteousness is a place of compassion and humility which is accessed through love and gratitude. It's never wrong to try to help those who suffer. However, suffering is necessary to crack open shells.

Battle Scars & Shedding Skins

What are soul contracts? Sacred agreements. We meet people here our souls recognize. We have experiences with them by which we gain valuable wisdom. We are tested. We become stronger. These are pre-agreements made in spirit.

Battle Scars & Shedding Skins

When the demon shows itself,
that's when the sword comes
out.

Battle Scars & Shedding Skins

Bleeding hearts...Maybe it's time to heal your wounds, rather than feed programs of anger, hate and fear with more anger, pain and fear.

Battle Scars & Shedding Skins

What I thought was missing in my
life through connection with others,
I discovered, was within me all along.
The sacred fire of initiation dissolved
my cocoon.

Battle Scars & Shedding Skins

In the graveyard of dreams, new experiences grow from thoughts planted with love.

Battle Scars & Shedding Skins

Treasure & Keys

We must make choices daily by 'judging' what is in our best interest, guided by our knowledge, experience, understanding, emotions, fears, wounds, etc., which is different from condemnation of others.

What is the energy which causes a person to feel it is in any way necessary or beneficial to put anyone else down through judgment or condemnation? Oh yeah…ego.

Treasure & Keys

Some say evil is ignorance. Demonstrated by how humanity is ignorant of its worthiness and magnificence. There is incompleteness.

Labels don't help. They are simply words to try to describe what is so difficult to understand. People learn through consequences from actions and free will choice.

Treasure & Keys

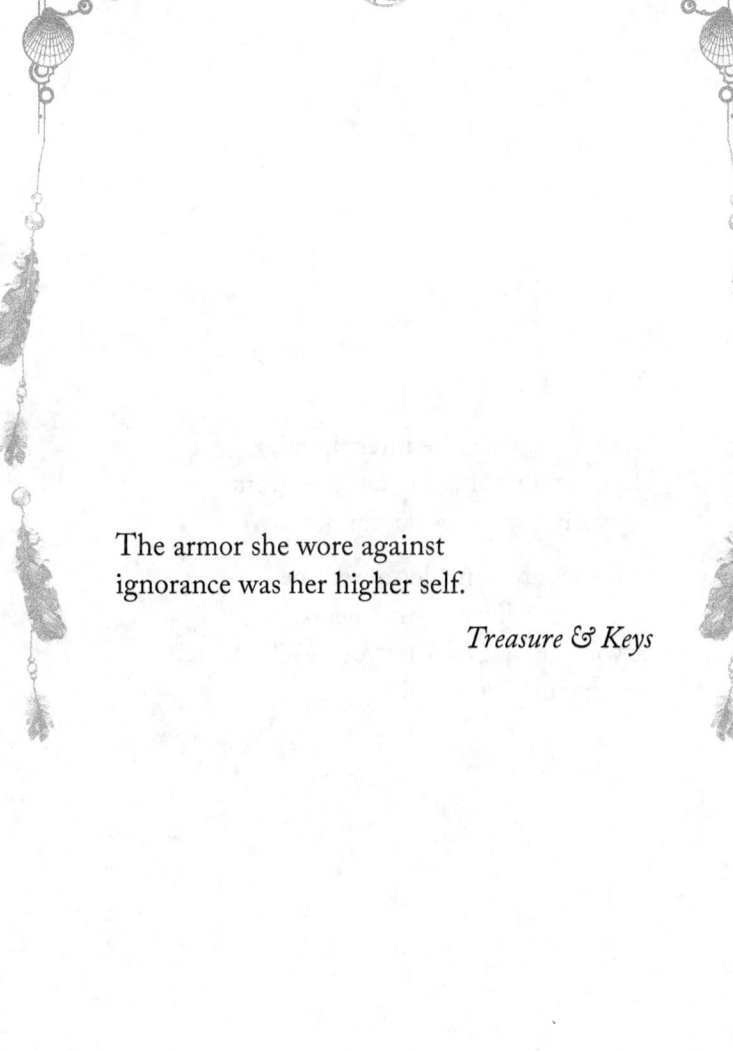

The armor she wore against
ignorance was her higher self.

Treasure & Keys

Don't let the kiss be interrupted.
Don't let anything distract you from
expressing what words cannot say.

Don't let any outside source keep
you from delivering the messages
of your heart. Don't let your soul's
agreement go unfulfilled.

Treasure & Keys

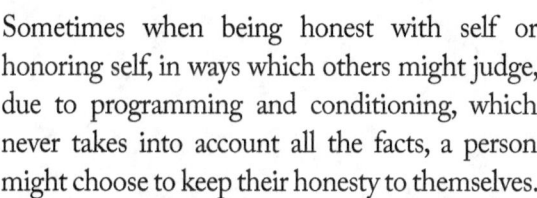

Sometimes when being honest with self or honoring self, in ways which others might judge, due to programming and conditioning, which never takes into account all the facts, a person might choose to keep their honesty to themselves.

They keep the manner in which they were honest with themselves and/or honored themselves to themselves, because others would call it dishonest and attempt to turn into a weapon to use against them.

It's like there are these self-righteous, egoic armies marching around looking for something or someone to condemn so they don't have to deal with or resolve their own issues, neither of which are fully understood at any time through the lens of illusion.

Allow the dragon's flame to burn away misperceptions and cords connecting us to ignorance, fear, jealousy, resentment, judgment, doubt, anger, guilt, grief, programming and unforgiveness. Truth to self is key. Forgiveness is key. Non-judgment is key. Compassion is the river which flows beautifully back to love.

Treasure & Keys

Judgments are limited and limiting.
We are tested to rise above them
or to move beyond them. It's all
choice.

Treasure & Keys

My vulnerability
became my strength

Treasure & Keys

Closeness between two beings, whether it's instant or whether it grows, is like coming home to the warmest welcome.

The voice of a beloved is a like a flame which warms the heart and kindles the fire of the soul.

Treasure & Keys

Suffering & Shadow

I've witnessed people who are 'good', behave in heinous, despicable, destructive, unkind, cruel ways, which often destroy relationships with people they love. WTH?

Suffering & Shadow

What is mind boggling is that people will swoop down upon you with their dark wings when you're in a weakened state. Punks preying on temporary weakness in an effort to gain false strength from the suffering or hardship of another, often created by them.

The darkness of their wings is from resentment, unforgiveness, self-doubt and lack of love.

Imagine their surprise when they must experience what they create. A vicious cycle of perpetrating wounds instead of healing them. It's all choice.

Suffering & Shadow

It seems that many so called Christians need to pull their heads out of certain places in order to see the light.

Maybe they should step out of fear and stop giving Satan so much power and credit. It's almost embarrassing.

Invisible shackles to be cut with one's own sword of truth.

Suffering & Shadow

So many collective egoic groups swimming in self-righteousness, judging others, feeding programs of stuck-ness. Not seeing God in everyone and everything.

How is that honoring God? It's all part of the learning experience. Swimming in illusion until we endeavor to rise above.

Suffering & Shadow

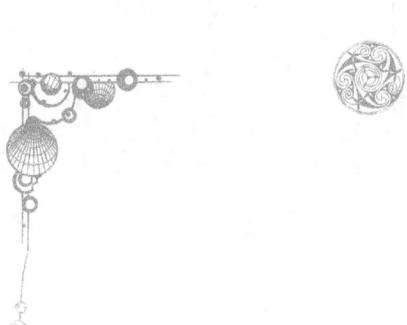

What he taught me through his great darkness, which I would not accept, strengthened me against it.

Suffering & Shadow

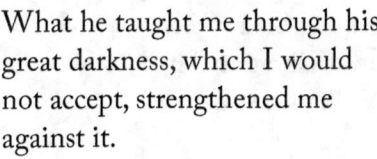

Judgment, anger and blame keep one stuck in lower vibrational hell. Rise above or walk out. Whenever you are ready, of course.

Suffering & Shadow

Light and Dark, Love and Fear

Light wouldn't know itself without dark and dark wouldn't know itself without light. They are part of the whole, opposite ends of the spectrum. Both of these are part of all of us and this reality we live in.

The Key is to find a balance between both, to be an observer and not get too drawn into one or the other in a position of feeling you are right or needing to defend it.

Your truth, which cannot be taken from you, does not need to be defended.

Just because someone believes something doesn't make it true. And just because they don't believe it doesn't make it false.

Truth is known, not believed.

Love opens and expands you; fear limits you and closes you off. What we face we can conquer, what we rise above we have conquered.

Suffering & Shadow

From a conversation with a friend. My friend knew a lady from her church, the Church of Jesus Christ of Latter Day Saints, aka the Mormon church. The lady went to visit her son and daughter-in-law in another state and while there, she attended church with them. It was another denomination of Christianity, supposedly. But then everything is up to interpretation or misinterpretation, whatever the case may be.

Apparently the pastor or whatever he would be called, knew the lady was coming to visit, and he was ready for her with a very un-Christian and unwelcome display of a holier-than-thou, ego demonstration, whereby he proceeded to vomit his ignorance and judgement all over her. He proceeded in attempting to make a spectacle out the Mormons, pointing out how 'wrong' their religion supposedly is for the benefit of his congregation, and to stroke his own ego in false righteousness. But in the end he only really succeeded in making a spectacle of himself. Very embarrassing, really. No church or religion is exactly right in its interpretations or misinterpretations of anything.

The lady remained composed and behaved like a civilized human being, unlike the poor excuse for a Christian posing as a pastor or preacher. That my friends, is how darkness works through religions and certain idiots in the grip of it seem to remain grossly unaware of their abominable behavior.

It doesn't matter what label of any particular denomination of religion or Christianity you plaster on yourself to try to fit into to some collective egoic group. You either honor God by example of how you treat your brethren or you possibly make a fool of yourself, often times even unbeknownst to you, and most likely thanks to programming and conditioning and a gross lack of compassion and intelligence.

After certain encounters with certain so-called Christians, some people be like, 'Let me just pull this knife out of my back…ah, that feels better.' And then throw it into the sacred fire. We are all tested here. None of us possesses all the wisdom or all the answers we want or need, but if we have compassion and humility, together or individually, we can make the world a kinder and better place. This is shared simply for awareness. Peace.

Suffering & Shadow

Whispers from the Heart

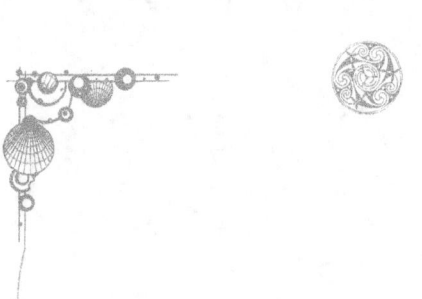

There comes a time to know
when what you have done is
enough.

Whispers from the Heart

Guilt might be fleeting or an unwelcome hitchhiker, but it must go. Don't carry it around like a sack of weight on your back. Guilty people often try to make others feel guilty because their burden is too much to carry.

That is when we talk to God or to our Angels and ask them to take the burden from us. When we recognize what we have learned, we can be in gratitude for the wisdom gained and we can give ourselves permission to release it. That is part of our self-care.

That is part of sweeping our temple floors. Help is always available to those who ask. Love yourself enough to release what does not serve you.

Whispers from the Heart

Sometimes you can't just crumble into a heap of despair and helplessness. Well, you can, but often those closest to you aren't even going to notice or know what to do, especially when they are used to you being the responsible one.

Sometimes strangers are kinder. Sometimes we try to take on too much at our own expense. We might crumble, but we are not meant to stay there. We can't get anything done there, except maybe to rest. We must rest to recuperate from life events, to process and release.

We might lie down in the grass and put our roots down to mingle with the trees and ask them to help us to heal, to release burdens. If we crumble, it's only temporary, because we have important work to do here. Coming to love ourselves again is part of it. When surrender happens, something shifts.

Whispers from the Heart

She had a deep and troubling question. What did one do when they loved a person for many reasons, but they couldn't love the demon that worked through the person, whatever that was? Whether it came through alcohol or drugs or through old unhealed wounds and shadow. When it was so cruel and destructive that she had to shove it out of her life with a warrior's force, and the nice side of person didn't want to go.

And many others weren't even aware of that side of the person because they didn't show it to everyone? She still didn't have the answer. The only solution for her was, that as long as the demon hitchhiker was there in a destructive capacity which had attacked her numerous times, she could not allow the person into her space or her life on any level of closeness or trust. Nothing personal. The experience only made her stronger and for that she was grateful.

Whispers from the Heart

Paths are always open to new beginnings, endings and opportunities to grow. They are boundless and limitless.

Whispers from the Heart

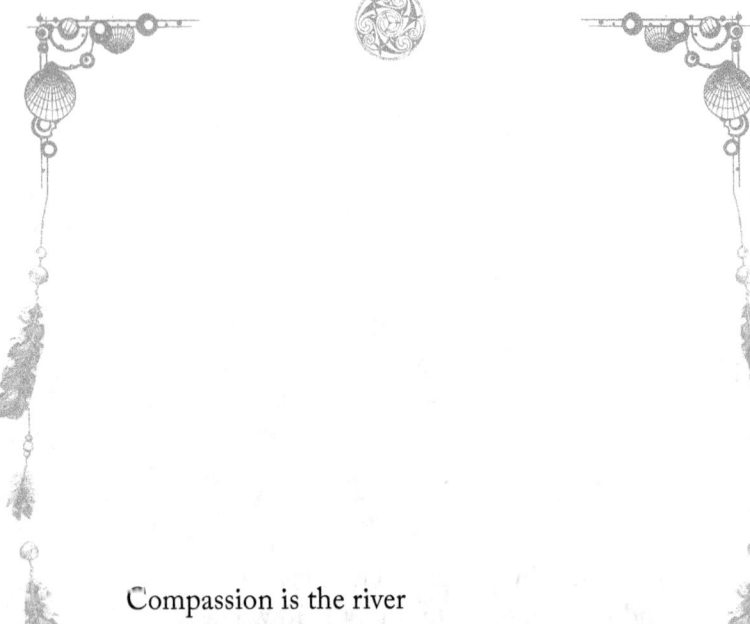

Compassion is the river
which flows back to love.

Whispers from the Heart

Light Through the Cracks

Sometimes the ones who did you wrong convince themselves they are in need of an apology from you, for some fabricated reason, (even if you already gave one), so they don't have to face all the reasons they really owe you an apology or apologies. They don't want to openly face, admit, acknowledge or speak about their heinous behavior. All their behavior was, is a snap-shot or replay or demonstration of abuse they endured in the past. Their unresolved or unhealed issues which they show you, they do in a way they don't realize will push most people far, far away.

When someone steps up to apologize it's important to hear it and recognize that it is a very humble thing to do. When someone is honest enough and open enough to admit something, apologize for it, discuss what they learned and new perspectives gained, that is huge, and it should be honored. If we cannot be open to that, then it might demonstrate something within us which needs to be addressed and healed.

Communication is a huge part of healing and sustaining relationships which isn't easy for everyone. Communication about growth and learning and kindness, and releasing what doesn't serve, elevates your vibration. That doesn't need to include talking shit about someone because we can't let something go. We can speak about people we've had experiences with in a respectful way, even if we don't understand it, or them or their behavior. Not communication of gossip, back biting and otherwise focusing on and spewing negativity because you feed off of it and it feeds off of you.

Shedding the cloak and chains of negativity isn't easy because it is connected to pain and loss and abuse and our perceptions of that. Our pain and experiences shouldn't define who we are. We might have survived things, but maybe we haven't survived ourselves or our thoughts about things. Cutting cords is powerful. Love and heal your inner child, which might be the one acting out when we do things to get negative attention.

Sometimes you work with people and hold space for them and say nice things to them and forgive them. However, when their unacceptable behavior doesn't stop, you may give yourself permission to walk away. You are not required to suffer abuse. You are not required to be dominated by negative energy that tries to pull you down into submission. The brave surrender to the light. Negativity reflects weakness, fear, anger. It is a low vibration. Bless those who are stuck there.

No blame. No shame. Only love, and that must include yourself.

Light through the Cracks

Tedium

The problem with Mr. Ego,
Is that we often don't know just when he rules,
We don't see our self-righteous behavior,
Trying to make others look like fools.

Oh high and mighty impostor,
Does that mask ever wear you down?
Are those puppet strings I see?
And who is the master clown?

Who runs the show of ignorance?
With peacock feathers as they fly?
In the face of cockiness?
Unseen by you and I?

Light through the Cracks

To try to understand him is folly. In order to do that I would have feel what he feels, to think what he thinks. To try to understand him might be to labor under misperception which might create more things to be healed through falsehood, illusion and misinterpretation.

Best to bless him where he is and walk away from what does not serve me and my highest good. It's my job to honor myself and to not be offended when others do not.

Light through the Cracks

Sometimes it's the guidance from the higher self which gets us through challenges. Strength from something unrecognized or unremembered.

Light through the Cracks

Sometimes we must cut things out of our lives which don't serve. Hopefully without judgment, just awareness.

Light through the Cracks

Thank you for cracking
me open to find my light.

Light through the Cracks

People help people in different ways, sometimes gentle, sometimes firm. Sometimes knowingly, sometimes unknowingly. It also comes down to the receptivity of the person needing help on whatever level.

Light through the Cracks

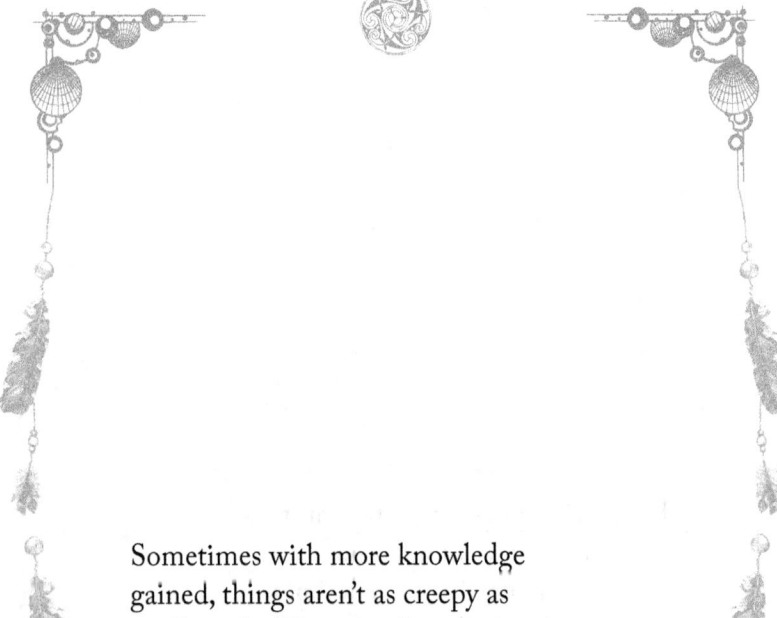

Sometimes with more knowledge gained, things aren't as creepy as we thought. There is often more or less to it.

Light through the Cracks

People often lash out at and attack what they don't understand or what they are jealous of. When you are raising your vibration and they're not, watch out!!

Light through the Cracks

Spoken from the Soul

What she contributed to his reality was so many things, which floated in an out, they changed in response to what was needed.

She changed in her roles like the changing of a hat. She put on the hat for what was needed. She was able to love in a way he had never experienced before.

He couldn't really describe what he felt for her, as his feelings went too deep. They went to places he felt he'd never been, places he wasn't sure he was ready to go. The weight of the walls around his heart might drown him if he dove in.

Spoken from the Soul

What you taught me through a perception of darkness I would not accept, was great power.

Spoken from the Soul

There was a wise and intuitive man who was my guide, teacher and friend. I thought of him as a sage. I learned from him and he learned from me. He was in need of healing, for his heart, as was I but for different reasons. I trusted him as a guide and as a friend. When the energy of his old wounds surfaced he went into a lower energy which proved to be destructive to our friendship, I had to pull away from that and when I did, I was told he spoke to others about me derogatorily.

It seemed his views were skewed, like he created things to be upset about which were not true and then he reacted to them. He told people things about me which were not true. He tried to turn some of my friends against me but wasn't completely successful as some of them were open and honest enough to see me for who I really am.

Some said they sensed jealousy in him. Jealousy is a diabolical, lower vibrational trap. Vindictiveness. Treachery. Dishonesty. Those are just labels to try to understand the behaviors of the wounded. He effectively damaged the relationship and the trust between us, later telling me he had trust issues.

I was being tested to get to a place where I no longer cared what people said or thought and to learn how to let go and rise above. Later he tried to mend things without being honest with himself about what he had done. The restoration can't happen without being honest with oneself. He was no longer a sage to me. I could no longer place that title upon an energy that would try so hard to harm me and then pretend it didn't happen.

Is a sage someone who would attempt on more than one occasion to hurt his student and friend? Methinks it's just a reflection of his unhealed wounds. Maybe that was actually part of the learning that was supposed to happen on levels I'm not fully aware of. I am grateful, however, for how the experiences with him strengthened me.

I now wear my sword on my back and I use it to cut away any negativity which does not serve me. I still have immense compassion, I just direct more of it toward myself now. When someone cannot bring themselves to do what is right by us, it's up to us to do so. We do it at least partially by telling our stories and sharing what wisdom was gained from them. We are not our stories, but they do shape us and redirect us.

Spoken from the Soul

Flowers speak with colors and energy what words could never say.

Spoken from the Soul

I've discovered the source and purpose of my warrior spirit, the drive to do what's right and good, even in the face of resistance. I have a messages to deliver. I have a calling. I have a mission. We all do. I lovingly and courageously accept mine. I am here to make a difference for the better, to reach, to inspire and to heal.

Spoken from the Soul

Trying to blame anyone but oneself
is often narcissistic. I've had some of
those as teachers. Some of the fiercest
battles of fuckery one can encounter.
Little trips through hell. But my flame
is mightier because of it.

Spoken from the Soul

People constantly react and
overreact to misinformation.

Spoken from the Soul

Roles. It's her higher self which guides her. She might wear armor and she might do the work of men sometimes and many people won't or don't understand that.

A warrior goddess whose magic is the balance between the divine feminine and the divine masculine in her/(him). Her higher self is her strength and wisdom, which sometimes reveals itself in ways even she doesn't understand.

Her higher self, she discovered, is different than she initially thought from her limited perspective of amnesia.

Spoken from the Soul

Beyond Belief

We are aspects of divinity in human form, here to resolve and fulfill contracts we don't remember. We play certain roles for what we will learn from those experiences, good or bad. There are things to unravel, to mend, to create, to weave, to love. It's all divinely orchestrated.

Beyond Belief

People are brave in many ways, known or unknown, seen or unseen. Many face and conquer things no one knows about. It is said that fear is a liar. Love is stronger than fear.

Beyond Belief

I love how when we step into our authenticity and attempt to do good works, people try to take us down. Not.

Beyond Belief

I Am more thankful for friends and teachers than I could ever say.

Beyond Belief

Sometimes our purpose here is simply to experience love, to give it and to receive it.

Beyond Belief

A belief which you adopt and stand by, for whatever reason, isn't necessarily truth or your truth.

If it is something of love without any fear, in which you know your worthiness and stand in your worthiness, then it is likely your truth.

If it instills or creates fear and if it makes you feel in any way unworthy, Then it is very likely not your truth.

Whenever we feel unworthy, we're disconnected from God/Source, Great Spirit, truth. What religion of any truth of the high God would promote or enforce a sense of unworthiness in any of God's beings? …An untrue one.

Or…Unworthiness comes from not recognizing ourselves or from not treating ourselves and our brethren and all beings with compassion.

Beyond Belief

When someone challenges your 'beliefs', they might seem challenged or opposed by people who have differing or limited information about it or who have had different experiences. What you know to be true for you, no one take from you. It does not need to be defended. Many feel they have to defend their beliefs. Often beliefs are not truth, perhaps only partial truths.

People feel they need to defend because they think someone is trying to take something from them. If it is your truth, no one can take it from you. Different levels of awareness doesn't make either of them wrong, just different while we are all in the process of learning and growing. If we keep an open mind our perspectives are always changing. If we don't, we stay stuck.

It's about allowing others to have their beliefs which might be limited or limiting, and walking away from anyone who doesn't allow you to have yours. No one can stop you from believing things, even if they don't believe them. No one can take away your truth.

Beyond Belief

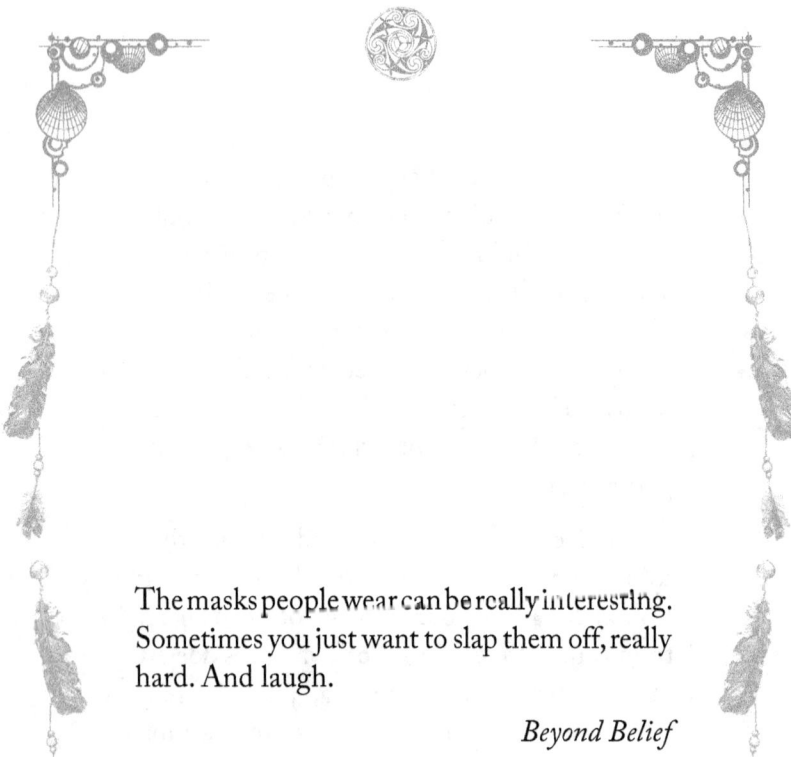

The masks people wear can be really interesting. Sometimes you just want to slap them off, really hard. And laugh.

Beyond Belief

She asked the cat, 'How am I supposed to read, if you are standing on my book?'

The cat said, 'Tell me a story.'

She began, 'There are times when the love felt between two beings is so strong, that it's painful. It's painful because it seems there is no proper way to fully express it. It's painful because distractions and events occur in life to test it, to harm it, to steal it or to destroy it.

It's beautiful and it's sad. It's uplifting and it's devastating. Sometimes choices must be made. Sometimes those choices are not for the person or for the love. It usually isn't, love or nothing. But love is in everything and everyone.

Just when we think things are turning out the way we dreamed, the rug gets pulled out from under us and we end up on the ground in the dust, in the mud from the dirt and our tears.

But in the end our heart is a safety net. In our hearts is the love we have always wanted and needed, and as we continue to give it away, it always finds its way back to us.'

As she gazed off into the distance, remembering, the cat reached out with a paw and gently touched her.

She said, 'Love is everywhere, if we look'

To the cat she said, 'The love you show me is a beautiful gift I am very thankful for.'

The cat purred because she knew love. She gave it and she received it, just like the story teller.

Beyond Belief

So many are afraid of what they don't understand in this realm of duality. Yes there is dark, and there is light, and there is also choice.

Beyond Belief

Metaphoric Light

What is church…? Sometimes it's about programming and conditioning and collective egoic groups identified with being right. Sometimes its control through fear.

Sometimes its true worship of God, whatever understanding that is to each individual. Sometimes It's about judging others and sometimes it's a connection of truth and love beyond judgment.

It's an ongoing unfoldment of grace in or out of church. It's how we treat our brethren. It's about the kingdom within. Church can be anywhere your heart and mind and spirit and soul are reflecting on the love of God which is in everyone and everything, beyond, jealousy and judgement.

Metaphoric Light

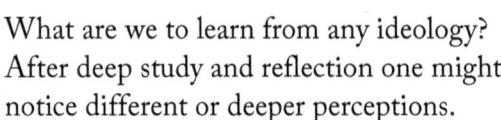

What are we to learn from any ideology? After deep study and reflection one might notice different or deeper perceptions.

After such on my personal and ongoing journey of discovery, I was at a church service where the bishop spoke of how we offend god and my first response to that was… 'Which god?'

It's important to come to a deeper level of understanding about what and who we worship and if the information we have to date in accurate and complete.

Being offended is of the ego. One would think that god would be above that. There are the good things churches and religions do, which must be acknowledged in gratitude.

And what should also be acknowledged is their gross misinterpretation of the word sin and how certain teachings are potentially very damaging to humanity.

Metaphoric Light

It's interesting when people fuck with the goddess or the dragon, not realizing who it is they are dealing with, and then the flame comes on and someone gets singed. Ouch. Lol.

Be aware of angels in disguise. Not everyone sees the flame. There is a difference between egoic cockiness and confidence of being when one awakens to who they are and why they are here.

Metaphoric Light

What messages from mirrors...
through mind or heart or soul?

Metaphoric Light

It's about shedding and peeling away
layers and layers of what doesn't serve,
to restore balance...

Metaphoric Light

The force of tides flowing in and out.
The call of something we can't quite
remember, something beautiful...

Metaphoric Light

If this world is ruled by beings which are or were ignorant of the fact that they are not the most high, does that make humans minions, if they have been kept in ignorance and false fear, guilt and shame…?

Metaphoric Light

Perspectives

It's thoughts about things which cause so much suffering. Be mindful of thought forms. Process and release. You are in charge of what thoughts are allowed to remain. Changing your thoughts will change the quality of your life. Perspective is key and perspectives are always changing with the addition of more knowledge.

Perspectives

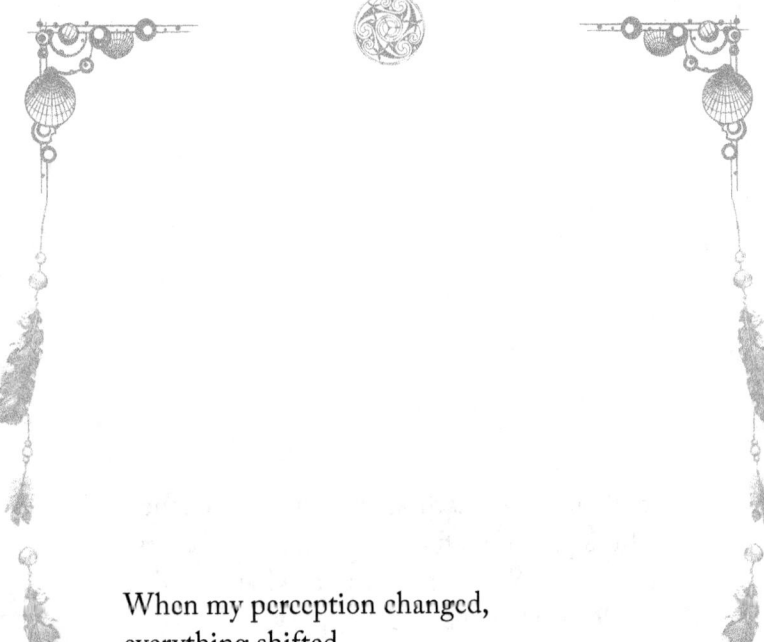

When my perception changed,
everything shifted.

Perspectives

Thank you for cracking me
open to find my light.

Perspectives

We can't accurately judge what anyone has been through, even if their stories about it trigger something in us.

Perspectives

I can see my progress, by my responses, or reactions, or lack thereof. Woohoo!!

Perspectives

The place for me is 'me', the expression of God through me, and what I bring to where I am and to those who recognize me, honor me, teach me, support me, remind me. I don't think or believe that I need anyone to make me happy, even though I have experienced it temporarily.

It was only temporary as it was karmic. When there is karma to be balanced there is intense love until it runs its course. We must find happiness where we are and in ourselves. There are many things woven together, intertwined, and many different vibrational levels, but they are all connected.

Through illusion, time, duality and free will choice we learn through suffering, until we gain the strength and wisdom to rise above it, usually out of our own ashes. A hot mess matrix of duality stew and an evolving experiment. Love is the highest truth. Peace.

Perspectives

People interpret things how they want to, or due to unreleased and unhealed programming and conditioning. Interpretation is only as accurate as the facts known, and all the facts are never known.

Perspectives

Feeding negativity with negativity and wondering why things don't change for the better. Is it sheer brilliance or a trap?

Perspectives

What do you feed your thoughts and energy into, positive or negative? How does it serve you?

Perspectives

A Discussion of Jealousy

Some feel that jealousy is a form of hatred built on insecurity. And so when someone does something terribly, unkind, inconsiderate or hurtful, what is our response to that supposed to be? It is normal to be wary of trusting anyone or anything again? So we create walls, armor and distance to protect ourselves. No matter how much we love someone.

Do we then not trust ourselves to be open to try it again? It's really difficult because of the pain it caused. Some wonder if it's worth putting your hand in the fire again. You are the fire.

People do things by their free will choice, right or wrong, but is our response or reaction to it which might create more pain and suffering. And what do we choose to carry?

Some believe that we make pre-agreements with people to have these very (horrific) experiences for how our souls will evolve, for what we will learn. It might seem unbelievable but we learn by experiencing, both sides of anything.

If we hold it against them we keep ourselves prisoner, to the situation, to the thoughts about it, to not letting it go. Sometimes people do things, unkind or uncaring because of their own unhealed issues. People try to fill a void that might be lacking self-love.

This is only a limited perspective but sometimes little bits of things filter through and might be helpful. So many people have immense walls and armor and suspect everyone to be the bad guy. If hearts are closed we can't heal. I was reminded by a shamanic healer to take better care of my inner child.

Perhaps much depends whether the lesson is learned so it can have a different outcome. I've had people do things which felt very hurtful and then I learned to detach to find peace.

I began to recognize the woundedness in those who wound. I have distanced myself from them, even though I still care about them. When I realized their atrocious and unacceptable behavior comes from unhealed parts of them, I didn't need to take it personally. They were huge tests and not easy.

I don't have to allow them in my space for their toxic bullshit to spew out all over the place, and I also don't need to carry it and allow it disrupt my energy or my peace. If we keep drinking that shit it keeps us in a lower vibration of bitterness and resentment. We are stronger than that. We just need to find the fortitude, to strengthen the weaknesses and heal the wounds.

Those wounded beings will often find those wounds and weaknesses and poke them and try to use them against you. It only has the power you give it. These are things I've learned along the way and I share them here in case anyone finds it helpful.

Some spiritual healers teach that when we give a lot of thought, especially negative thought to anything, it creates an energetic entity which sticks to our energy field and must be fed—its fed by the negative thought loops we continually replay. We run programs. If we can identify and become aware of what programs we are running, we can release them. We need to clear that debris out of our energetic space. If we don't it can create dis-ease. Release what does not serve.

If a person studies the Gnostic Gospels about the origin of the world, etc., they begin to learn about what rules this planet, and about ignorance–meaning something is lacking or incomplete on a spiritual level and thereby jealousy, wrath, etc., is born. Maybe earth school is a grueling test to rise above. These experiences are part of the initiations.

Many believe we create heaven or hell here, now, by our choices, decisions, actions and reactions. If we don't like something we have created, we can change it. Only we can do it for ourselves. Acceptance and surrender come into play to be able to move beyond. I learned from a spiritual teacher that if I accept that this is the way things are right now, then I can determine what I want to do next to change it or move beyond. But if we resist and resent, we can't move forward.

Jealousy seems to be a poison people don't realize they drink. Many people can see it very clearly in the behavior of others but often are not be able to say anything to the person because it would be denied and rejected.

When people constantly suspect other people of doing things they are not doing, it's very unfair. When they believe things which are not true, they suffer and cause many others to suffer as well. Perpetuating the cycle of suffering. It happens every day and with people we know and call friends.

Sometimes we hold space for friends and we question whether we should. Sometimes shutting out the wounded due to bad behavior doesn't help the situation. They are tests. We don't need to tolerate disrespectful behavior, but when we realize it's not about us, that changes the entire perspective.

As with anything, one might ask the question, 'How does jealousy serve me?' But if they don't realize they are jealous or continue to deny it, then the cycle continues in a downward spiral or stuckness.

There is something called secondary gains. We often check for this in energy healing work and hypnotherapy. It is when someone is getting something by holding onto a problem. Like if they keep talking about it and focusing on it and are getting attention from that.

Sometimes those who try to love us when we are stuck in that pain fail because they feel like they fail all the tests...because we shut them out.

There is a saying, the bitter heart eats its owner and that unforgiveness is like drinking poison and expecting another to suffer. We do need to process and that might take a while, as long or as short as it takes, for us to take our power back.

It's difficult when we don't understand why something happened and when it feels like we didn't matter to people we care about. Sometimes we don't need to understand, we just need to let go and let it go. It is so important to love yourself and to forgive yourself. We cannot forgive others if we don't forgive self.

Perspectives

About the Author

JANINE PALMER (SPIRIT SILVER MOON) grew up in Northern California and resides in Utah today. After devastating county-wide wild fires in Southern California and global economic collapse, Janine and her family endured physical, economical and emotional losses, along with the loss of friendships. Judgmental treatment by so-called religious people (family/friends) caused her to question religions due to poor treatment by others in religious ideology. These initiations tested her inner strength and caused her to investigate more deeply for truth, what brings true happiness, forward movement, the evolvement of the soul and ultimately she discovered her calling.

She was a phoenix who rose from her own ashes with a powerful story to share of truth, strength, wisdom, compassion, love and taking one's power back. We must remember our magnificence to in order to rise above so much illusion. Looking for answers, Janine Palmer (Silver Moon) extensively studied and continues to study multiple healing modalities for emotional and spiritual healing.

Janine has studied World Religions, Spirituality, Early Christianity, Gnosticism, Philosophy, Critical Thinking, Biblical Scholars, and Spiritual teachers. Janine is a Clinical Hypnotherapist and Shamanic Practitioner. In the spiritual and emotional arenas, Janine has studied and become certified in the following areas: Cognitive Behavioral Hypnotherapy, Ericksonian Hypnosis, Energy Psychology, Emotional Freedom Technique (EFT or Tapping), Kinesiology, Muscle Testing, Neuro-linguistic Programming (NLP) the language of the mind, Reiki Master and Gamma Healing for overcoming energy vampires, healing emotional traumas, anxiety, depression and PTSD, and Shamanic Journey Work.

These modalities are helpful for releasing stress, old pain, resentment, anger, doubt, grief, unforgiveness or anything which blocks forward movement. Through her healing sessions, whether held in person, via phone or skype, she has helped others heal, grow, overcome obstacles and move forward lighter after releasing what no longer serves. This knowledge and wisdom is contained within her writings of uplifting messages for healing. She shares tools we can use to assist ourselves and others on their path. Janine is the author of multiple books containing many genres and messages from various teachings and modalities. The four main genres are story poems, romance, rising above dogma and emotional and spiritual healing. These are presented as poetic tales which have received very positive support and feedback around the world.

Janine's compassion and calling to help others break free of limiting and painful situations can be felt through the writings contained her he book series Divine Heretic. She does God's work for humanity, for the collective and greater good. It is a gift and a blessing she is very grateful for.

Visit Janine's web pages

www.HarmonyEnergyHealing.com

www.DivineHereticBooks.com

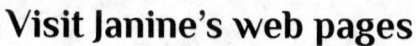

www.ingramcontent.com/pod-product-compliance
Lightning Source LLC
Chambersburg PA
CBHW052021070526
44584CB00016B/1847